DAVID'S BOOK OF LETCHWORTH

David's
BOOK OF LETCHWORTH
FIRST GARDEN CITY

A Brief History & Practical Guide by
ROGER HARRISON *with* DAVID WALKER

DAVID'S BOOKSHOPS, LETCHWORTH

Published by David's Bookshops (Letchworth) Ltd
14 Eastcheap, Letchworth Garden City, Hertfordshire SG6 3DE
www.davids-bookshops.co.uk
© 2006 Roger Harrison & David Walker

ISBN 0-9554333-0-4
ISBN 978-0-9554333-0-6

We gratefully acknowledge the assistance of Kenneth Johnson in reading
the text for factual errors. Any that remain are our responsibility.

Photographs: Sarah Davies
Maps: Paul Palmer
Design: Iain Bain

Historic photographs courtesy of the First Garden City Heritage
Museum, Letchworth

COVER ILLUSTRATION *from* 'Letchworth Garden City', linocut poster
by Lynn Evans. Reproduced courtesy of Letchworth Museum
& Art Gallery

FRONTISPIECE: The First Garden City Heritage Museum. Built in 1907,
it was the drawing office of Barry Parker and Raymond Unwin, winners
of the competition to design the new Garden City. The two-storey
extension was added by Barry Parker in 1937 as his home

Printed in Great Britain
by S.G. Street & Co Ltd, Royston Road
Baldock, Hertfordshire SG7 6NW

CONTENTS

Why another Letchworth book?

Letchworth Garden City's centenary in 2003 gave the town one of its periodic moments in the national spotlight. The BBC arrived to broadcast Any Questions and Songs of Praise, and articles in the national press assessed the role of the Garden City. Not all comment was favourable – *The Times* thought Letchworth's suburban ethos had reinforced the British tendency to petit-bourgeois prissiness. However the *Guardian* considered Letchworth's human scale to be far more attractive than many more modern developments. John Prescott, deputy prime minister, visited the town in June 2004 and pronounced it 'a role model for future development'.

The centenary was a reminder of the continued relevance of many of the issues that prompted the foundation of the Garden City movement – overcrowding in big cities, the availability of affordable housing, the environment. Increasingly we are questioning frenetic lifestyles and the work/life balance. All these concerns would have been recognised by the pioneer Edwardian colonists who first arrived on the green field site of Letchworth Garden City.

This book is intended as a guide to the town and its area, with information on what to do and see and some suggested walks to give a feel for the Garden City. There is a bit on history and on the economics of the Garden City, particularly the unique way in which the principle of the 'unearned increment' has worked to the eventual benefit of the town, as well as on the role of the Letchworth Garden City Heritage Foundation, the custodian of the inheritance of Ebenezer Howard, Letchworth's founder.

The definitive work on Letchworth, written in 1989 and updated in 2002, is Dr Mervyn Miller's *Letchworth – The First Garden City*. Heather Elliott and John Sanderson have produced two charming volumes, *Letchworth Recollections* and *Letchworth Reminiscences* from tape recorded interviews with inhabitants covering the periods 1903-1930 and 1930-1960, and a third volume is in preparation. Ken Johnson's lively 1975 *Book of Letchworth* remains a popular local history. Abundant information on the town and the town planning movement is to be found at Letchworth Library in Broadway while the Heritage Museum in Norton Way South has many original source materials.

The Garden City of Letchworth has had as much influence on the way we live now as any of the great inventions of the 20th century. What Howard and those who worked with him did was to transform the aspirations of ordinary people and to prove that it was possible for everyone to live in decent, clean and pleasant surroundings. That outcome was not at all inevitable at the end of the 19th century when Howard began his crusade. If we now take our semi-detached houses, our gardens and our green spaces for granted, if they are ordinary and unexceptional, it is because Howard and the pioneers made them the norm.

There was inspiration too from the founders of the Arts and Crafts movement, who taught us to take pride in ordinary things and to make them beautiful, and who had a strong influence on early Letchworth architecture. Later housing may lack the picturesque gables and dormer windows, inglenooks and porches with bench seats characteristic of the Arts and Crafts style, but for many of the working people who moved into Pixmore Avenue, Wilbury or, after the Second War, the Grange or Jackmans estates, the new houses were dramatic improvements on what had gone before – clean, spacious, easy to maintain, with inside toilets, bathrooms and modern kitchens. They too play their part in demonstrating how town planning moved on from the first ideas through the middle decades of the 20th century.

The book closes with a brief assessment of where the Garden City principles now stand and what they can still offer those in search of solutions to problems of housing and development versus the environment, or those searching for alternative lifestyles.

Early Days Remembered

From an interview with Garden City pioneer Mrs Barry Parker, widow of the Letchworth architect and planner Barry Parker, in 1969

'Anyone coming to Letchworth now would find it difficult to understand. There were 227 people here when I first came, nearly all farmers and farm workers. When development started there was nothing here at all; one had to shop in Hitchin and there wasn't even a station.'

'Women had nowhere to meet. We got together and had working parties and got some money. The Mrs Howard Memorial Hall was put up as the only place we could meet for anything. We wanted everybody to feel welcome. No class distinction – that was a very fundamental thing.'

'We had to do everything ourselves. There was a pioneering feeling in working together. It was frightfully exciting and enormous fun.'

'There was hardly any evening when there wasn't something going on. I saw little of my husband; he was out every evening.'

'We wanted their children to know hygiene. There were prizes for the best kept cottages. I was one of the judges.'

'We were a small community but we got such interesting people here. We had visits from Bertrand Russell, HG Wells, Bernard Shaw, Edward Carpenter and others. A lot of the outstanding people from the beginning of this century came down to lecture and stay.'

'It was a most inspiring and fulfilling period of time. Always thinking things and doing things. Many people coming here found a spirit of "something worthwhile to do".'

'My husband spent his life more or less apologising because he never had the standards he wanted. The directors would let the plots to anyone who would take them. Barry had to compromise tremendously over the standards.'

'Are the ideals being fulfilled? I would say fundamentally yes – the ideals to bring industry and workers into the country to live in conditions of pure air in a good home.'

'Ebenezer Howard we knew very well. He was a family man; he wanted the working man to get home to dinner in the middle of the day, not to be divorced from the family. He wanted children to go out with jam jars and catch tiddlers – to be in touch with the country.'

'In Hitchin the feeling was we were very inferior people. Socially we didn't exist. People would look down on you if you came from Letchworth.'

PART ONE

A Brief History

1. In the Beginning

What is now the Garden City has been occupied since prehistoric times. The ancient Icknield Way runs through the north of the town. Neolithic remains have been found in Works Road, including part of a 20-metre diameter ring ditch and a cluster of pits containing the remains of piglets and lambs, as well as parts of a large aurochs cow, a species thought to have become extinct almost 4,000 years ago. Also found was a grave, probably medieval.

Just off Stotfold Road, near the junction with Icknield Way on the other side of the road from the Wilbury Hill picnic area, is a late bronze age (1000-750 BC) hill fort believed to have been occupied throughout the Iron Age and at various times during the Roman period. It is one of six similar hill forts sited at regular intervals along the northern Chilterns.

At High Avenue finds of broken but well-preserved Roman pottery and other debris, including oyster shells, roof tiles and iron scrap, suggest there was once a modest working settlement with a wide range of trade links, which reached its peak during the 4th century AD.

Slightly further afield, there have been rich finds in Baldock, especially alongside Clothall Road. Letchworth Museum in Broadway has an excellent collection from these various excavations.

All three villages that make up modern Letchworth appear in the Domesday Book: Letchworth itself as Leceworde, Norton as now, and Willian as Wilie. The church of St Mary the Virgin in Letchworth Lane, old Letchworth, is a combination of 12th, 13th and 15th century building, St Nicholas church in Norton was dedicated in 1119, and All Saints Church in Willian dates back to around 1150.

In Willian, a much larger village in medieval times before the Black Death struck in the 14th and 15th centuries, earthworks show the sites of earlier houses and enclosures, especially near the pond on the north side of the road, with the line of a large, hollow way and several enclosures and raised house platforms. Take the footpath opposite the Fox and, keeping the pond on your left, follow it up a gradual slope and the earthworks are all around you.

In the 19th century, Willian was substantially remodelled by the local land-

◄ The original Letchworth parish church, St Mary's in Letchworth Lane, which dates from the 12th century

The village of Letchworth had a population of about 100 before the Garden City began. These old cottages in Letchworth Lane are at its heart.

Norton was one of the three villages that were absorbed into the Garden City. It was larger than Letchworth, with a population of about 170. This thatched cottage is on its outskirts.

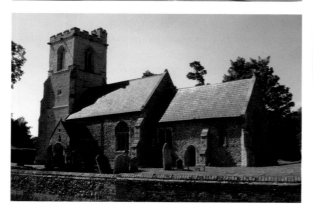

The church of All Saints at Willian dates back to around 1150.

owner. The main route through the village, past what is now the back of the Fox and the church, was diverted to provide the picturesque grouping of church, pub, green and pond that we know today.

By the start of the 20th century, Norton had a population of about 170; Letchworth around 100, and Willian around 300.

2. A TOWN IS BORN

A little over 100 years ago a few cottages and houses began to appear on the farmland between the little villages of Letchworth and Norton in north Hertfordshire. The Garden City adventure was under way.

Near the Hitchin-Cambridge railway line, workmen constructed great sheds for themselves as a depot and living quarters and began to dig to install drains and gas pipes and lay out new roads. Soon houses were forming a ring round the Norton common, and larger homes were springing up by the Hitchin to Baldock road. A railway halt with wooden platforms enabled Londoners to visit the new houses. Alongside the railway, factories started to grow, and with them came more people and more houses. Between the wars, great factories like palaces appeared and workers came by bus and by cycle from neighbouring towns. Training centres took in men from depressed areas, boosting the population, while the end of the second war saw a further influx of refugees and displaced Londoners. There were more schools and a college, and, when the industries hit hard times, a new motorway and newly electrified railway made working in London easier. The town lost its heavy industry but gained two high chimneys to compensate. The original college made way for a supermarket, some factories and schools were replaced by more shops and houses, and some ugly office blocks were turned into more handsome office blocks.

Behind it all was the vision of one man, Ebenezer Howard, the inspiration behind Letchworth Garden City.

Tomorrow in Context

When Howard, a parliamentary reporter, published his little manifesto *Tomorrow – a Peaceful Path to Real Reform* in 1898, he addressed widespread concerns about the social conditions of the great Victorian cities.

The cities were an increasing source of pride, with their theatres, galleries and parks. Their councils invested in libraries and institutes. New universities were founded. There were grand public buildings, while railways and tramways allowed people from the spreading suburbs to travel to the centre for work, business, entertainment and shopping.

Yet teeming slums abounded. Overcrowding and bad sanitation led to disease, crime and deprivation. The cities were socially divided. Above all, there was pollution, as coal-fired industrial plant and household heating belched out smoke. Fog and poor air quality were normal.

Rural dwellers, meanwhile, their jobs eroded by the mechanisation of farming, had faced a new threat – the imports of staples such as grain and meat from abroad – after railways and ocean-going ships had opened up the empire and North America. People flocked to the towns to escape rural poverty, adding to overcrowding while the countryside suffered from depopulation.

There were great advances in education and public health. Democracy developed, with the establishment of universal suffrage for men. There came an acknowledgment that the state would play a more important part in creating a better life.

In art and culture, there was a reaction to what some saw as the ugliness of modern life. This was reflected in the growth of the aesthetic movement and the Arts and Crafts movement, led by William Morris, with its insistence that common things – the furnishing of our homes, tools and machines used at work – could be objects of pleasure as much as of function.

There were fears as well. Karl Marx had written his critique of capitalism, there were outbreaks of revolutionary fervour in continental Europe. Would England face violent revolution?

Ebenezer Howard thought he had an answer – a way to eliminate the urban slums, end rural poverty and create a decent life for ordinary people while avoiding the threat of violence. And with *Tomorrow – a Peaceful Path to Real Reform*, he set out his manifesto for change.

Born in London in 1850, Howard was educated in Suffolk, tried farming in the American West, and then settled in London as clerk to the political reporting firm of Gurneys. In the parliamentary debates he listened to politicians wrestling with the social problems of both the cities and the countryside and wondered whether politicians were the people best fitted to resolve them.

Tomorrow's 130-odd pages are a near perfect example of how to communicate complex ideas in a simple way. There is nothing dense or particularly scholarly. That is surely one reason for the fact that within five years – with a second edition of the book in 1902 under the new title of *Garden Cities of Tomorrow*

Ebenezer Howard, the visionary who conceived the idea of the Garden City and achieved the backing to turn it into reality. His early home in Norton Way South (above) was designed by Parker and Unwin. He later moved to Homesgarth, now Sollershott Hall.

– his dream had been translated into reality. A major principle, the Three Magnets, was explained in one diagram. Many of the funding calculations are in almost back-of-an-envelope style. Howard recognised the practicalities – he was no dreamy utopian – but his main concern was the broad outline. Other influential and talented people joined in to clothe the skeleton with flesh.

Howard argued that the problems of town and country were the most urgent of the day. People were often divided, he said, on social issues such as temperance, religion or the opium trade. 'There is, however, a question in regard to which one can scarcely find any difference of opinion. It is well-nigh universally agreed by men of all parties, not only in England, but all over Europe and America and our colonies, that it is deeply to be deplored that people should continue to stream into the already over-crowded cities, and should thus further deplete the country districts.' London presented the biggest problems. Howard quoted Lord Rosebery as Chairman of the London County Council (1891): 'Sixty years ago a great Englishman, Cobbett, called it (London) a wen. If it was a wen then, what is it now? A tumour, an elephantiasis sucking into its gorged system half the life and the blood and the bone of the rural districts.'

Howard then considered the advantages and disadvantages of living in the town and the country and proposed a blend of the best elements of both, without the disadvantages of either, in his analysis of the Three Magnets:

THE THREE MAGNETS

BAD	*GOOD*
TOWN	
Closing out of nature	Social opportunity
Isolation of crowds	Places of amusement
Distance from work	High money wages
High rents and prices	Chances of employment
Excessive hours	Well lit streets
Army of unemployed	Palatial edifices
Fogs and droughts	
Foul air, murky sky	
Slums and Gin palaces	
COUNTRY	
Lack of society	Beauty of nature

Hands out of work	Wood, meadow, forest
Land lying idle	Fresh air
Long hours, low wages	Trespassers beware
Lack of drainage	Low rents
Lack of amusement	Abundance of water
No public spirit	Bright sunshine
Need for reform	
Crowded dwellings	
Deserted villages	

TOWN-COUNTRY

This third magnet would offer the advantages of each, with none of the disadvantages:

Beauty of nature	Freedom
Fields and parks of easy access	Social opportunity
	High wages
Low rents	Plenty to do
Low rates	No sweating
Low prices	Flow of capital
Field for enterprise	Good drainage
Pure air and water	No smoke, no slums
Bright homes and gardens	Co-operation

The novel part of Howard's proposal is the method of financing the new town. This would be by capturing the 'unearned increment' – the increase in land value that accrued when agricultural land was developed for housing. Normally this would pass to the landlord, as it already did in the cities. However, in the garden city, since the landlord would be the Garden City company, rates would be payable to it, and would be used entirely for the benefit of the community. That way, the start-up capital and any interest on it would be paid, with a surplus for civic services and amenities. The company would have shareholders, but their investment return would be limited to 5 per cent, with any surplus used to develop the town for the benefit of its citizens.

Howard emphasised the non-political nature of his proposals. As Charles Purdom, the garden city company's first agent on site when work started and later a participant in and commentator on the wider town planning movement, wrote: 'Almost everyone could see something in it that he liked.' Socialists would approve of the municipal nature of the scheme, Conservatives that it allowed private enterprise to develop the project, and Liberals would appreciate the land reform ideas. The principle of the unearned increment 'violated no political or economic principles, and had no opponents'.

The Garden City and its Precursors

Letchworth Garden City was not the first attempt to create an ideal settlement. But others were mostly sponsored by enlightened industrialists concerned to provide good housing for employees. Robert Owen established New Lanark in Clydesdale in the 1830s; Titus Salt built his mill and surrounding town, on a modern gridiron pattern, on the river Aire at Saltaire in the 1850s. The first of Letchworth's immediate predecessors was Port Sunlight on the Mersey, founded by John Lever in 1893, which revived the Cheshire Tudor style in its streets of half-timbered cottages. In 1896, George Cadbury established Bournville to the south of Birmingham. Cadbury, however, intended Bournville to be socially mixed, so for the first time the homes were intended for the public at large and not exclusively for employees. One of the other Quaker chocolate families, the Rowntrees, also commissioned cottage-style housing for their employees in York at the turn of the century, employing a partnership of young architects, Barry Parker and Raymond Unwin.

Letchworth was, however, the first that did not aim to provide housing for established factories; indeed it would have to attract factories to succeed. It was owned not by individual philanthropists but by a company, with the object of developing the site for all citizens. It was therefore a communitarian venture, something new.

Both Lever and Cadbury were to help Howard in the promotion of his project. Howard's book, followed up by a series of lectures, made a rapid impact and by June 1899 he was in a position to form the Garden Cities Association with the express purpose of putting his ideas into practice. Its objective was 'To promote the discussion of the projects suggested by Mr Ebenezer Howard in *Tomorrow* and ultimately to formulate a practicable scheme on the lines of that project'. The Association was careful to draw membership from a wide range of society and had a membership fee of one shilling. Supporters included MPs from all parties, members of the London County Council and luminaries such as the writer George Bernard Shaw. The appointment in 1901 of the barrister Ralph Neville as Chairman, and a surveyor, Thomas Adams, as Secretary further stimulated the activity of the Association. Adams, who possessed a talent for public relations, persuaded George Cadbury to host a national conference at Birmingham in September 1901 to debate the need for affordable working class housing, the need to attract industry, and above all the means of retaining the unearned increment within the community.

On June 2 1902, the Association formed the Garden City Pioneer Company to seek and purchase a site for the model city. It was to be funded with working capital of £20,000. Cadbury, Lever and Neville subscribed £1,000 each. A number of possible sites were examined, and by autumn 1902 the favourite appeared to be the Chartley Castle estate near Stafford. However, the Company's solicitor, Herbert Warren, who had purchased a business in Baldock, together with Neville and Warren's assistant James Brown, became aware of the possibility of purchasing the Alington estate at Letchworth. By adding various other parcels of land between Baldock and Hitchin, an estate of sufficient size for the intended city could be created. Because the purchase price was more affordable than the Chartley site (at £155,587, it was only just over Howard's suggested target price of £40 per acre) and because of its proximity to London, Letchworth was chosen.

The Company formed First Garden City Limited, which was registered on September 1 1903, with an authorised share capital of £300,000. The estate was formally opened by Earl Grey, the patron of the Garden City movement, on October 9 in a marquee on the south side of Baldock Road where the Tennis Club now is. Legend has it that the ceremony took place in pouring rain, though a Hertfordshire Express report says the rain had ceased by that Friday. Either way, it was sufficiently wet for the lane leading to the marquee to be christened Muddy Lane, the name it has retained. An eight-mile hike around the bound of the estate to Willian, Norton and Wilbury Hill was offered to the guests.

Town Planning Begins

The company held a competition to decide on a plan. Three designs were shortlisted, all featuring Howard's 'town-country' principle, with spacious layouts and prominent centres as focal points. None, however, followed Howard's idea of concentric circles – there are no orbital railway, central park or crystal malls. The planners sited industry alongside the existing Great Northern railway line rather than on the edges. The practicalities of the topography of the site and other influences such as the fashion for the American gridiron pattern, modified by diagonals as in Paris and Barcelona, took precedence in the designers' agendas.

The opening of the Co-operative Stores in Leys Avenue in 1907.

Star Supply Stores, a chain of grocers who apparently gave money away. Leys Avenue, c.1910.

Alpha Cottages in Baldock Road, the first houses built in the fledgling Garden City. Parker and Unwin were critical of their off the shelf design.

Of the two plans that did not win, that by W R Lethaby and Halsey Ricardo envisaged a rectangular layout between Icknield Way and Baldock Road, with a town centre on the east side of the Pix brook, roughly in the location of the present Hillshott School. The main focal point would have been a central square with a bell-tower and a main north-south road running through. Industry would have been located in the north east corner of the site. The other, by a partnership of Sydney Cranfield and a young Hitchin architect, Geoffry Lucas, shows a fairly rigid gridiron pattern, modified with hexagonal and octagonal squares. The town would have been built between Norton Road and Baldock Road, using the railway as a central axis and with industry grouped around the railway. This, though, was seen as a decisive drawback as it would have divided the town's residential areas into two. Cranfield and Lucas's town centre would have been slightly to the east of the present one, near the Pix brook.

The winners were two architect brothers-in-law from Buxton in Derbyshire, Barry Parker and Raymond Unwin, whose design was adopted on February 11 1904. They featured a central square with a radial system of streets. Though never fully completed, it is essentially the Letchworth we know today, but with clear differences such as the Pixmore area and the layout to the north-west, where the diagonal of Bedford Road was missing.

The first houses built by the company, using local Hitchin builders, Picton and Hope, were Alpha Cottages, which still stand at the corner of Baldock Road and Norton Way North. The first inhabitant, Miss Elizabeth Harriett Revill, moved in on July 7 1904. These were soon followed by a group of cottages in Paddock Close designed by Parker and Unwin, who were critical of the 'off the shelf' design of Alpha Cottages.

Early Letchworth was designed round the then existing east-west routes of the Hitchin-Baldock road, Icknield Way and Wilbury Road, with the unpaved tracks of Dunhams Lane, Green Lane and Spring Road the only north-south routes. Labourers from London were housed in sheds north of the present railway station and were employed in laying out the infrastructure of new roads with their gas mains and sewers as well as the buildings themselves. Due to lack of finance, progress was halting, but things accelerated in 1905 with the opening of a first railway station, just west of the present location, on April 15, and the launch of the Cheap Cottages Exhibition. This innovative project challenged builders and architects to build affordable houses for agricultural workers (rather than the urban workers the town was aiming at) at a maximum price of £150. During the summer of 1905 34,000 people came by train, mostly from London, to see the results, most of which are still standing in Nevells

Road (then known as Exhibition Road) and either side of Norton Common in Icknield Way and Wilbury Road.

The Cheap Cottages were a remarkable advertisement for the Garden City, demonstrating Howard's principles that housing could be attractive yet afford-able. Combined with the green spaces much in evidence, an altogether more congenial lifestyle beckoned the would-be colonist.

Howard envisaged a ring of garden cities, with good transport links both between each of them and between them and a central city, making possible amenities beyond the reach of a single town. As the new garden cities took population out of the great industrial cities, he believed, the pressures on them would lessen, slums could be cleared and a better life made possible there too. The Government-sponsored post-war new towns and the slum clearance schemes in the old cities owe much to this dream.

3. THE GROWTH OF AN IDEAL

Democracy and the Economy

From the outset, there was a tension between the company and the local au-thority. Howard had recommended elections for executive posts in the Board of Management but this was never implemented. So there was no democratic mandate. The local authority in 1903 was Hitchin Rural District Council. A Residents Union was established in July 1905 – one of the first organisations in Britain to be appointed through full adult suffrage. A parish council was set up in March 1908, and an urban district council in 1919, with powers over planning and building rights.

Because local authorities could borrow on better terms, it was cheaper for the RDC and then the UDC to build houses than it was for the company. Even in the early days the company tended to leave the building of houses to others, whether housing associations or private builders, making its money from the sale of leases – houses were sold leasehold, with a ground rent payable to the company, rather than freehold.

Because the eventual intention was for ownership of the town to revert to its inhabitants, with shareholders required to give up their stake, the company had difficulty raising sufficient start-up capital. Even the prospect of a 5 per cent a year return was by no means guaranteed. Any capital gain would pass to the inhabitants, as stated in the prospectus for the town:

24